ANIMAL AND MAN IN BIBLE LANDS

ANIMALS FROM THE MURAL PAINTINGS OF TEILEILAT GHASSUL. (See p. 155).

Above: Fox? The triangle behind it is almost certainly an independent ornament.

Below: Gazelle?

COLLECTION DE TRAVAUX DE L'ACADEMIE INTERNATIONALE D'HISTOIRE DES SCIENCES

N° 10

ANIMAL AND MAN IN BIBLE LANDS

BY

Dr F. S. BODENHEIMER

Late Professor of Zoology, Hebrew University, Jerusalem

FIGURES AND PLATES

LEIDEN
E. J. BRILL
1972

Original title

שמעון בודנהיימר, החי בארצות המקרא·

תולדות בעלי החיים בארץ־ישראל ושכנותיה מתקופת האבן ועד לסוף תקופת המקרא·
בלוויית לוחות וציורים
מוסד ביאליק ירושלים תש״י·

Translation by the Author

ISBN 90 04 03541 9

CONTENTS

FIGURES

6. Natufian Gazelle Sculpture discovered by R. Neuville in the Umm Qatafah cave. The missing head of the fawn is reconstructed from a similar sculpture from Uruk (Heinrich, Uruk, 1936).

7. Neolithic Rock Carvings from Kilwa:

1 — Sacrifice (?) of ibex with adorant man.
2 — Wounded ibex with arrow and adorant man.
3 — Cattle, two ibexes, dog and crouching man.
4 — Ibex and dromedary.
5 — Dromedary.
6 — Ibex herd.
(Completely redrawn from Rothert, 1938).

8. Nabathaean Rock Carvings from Kilwa:

1 — Scene of ibexes and dogs.
2 — Ibex and dog.
3 — Ibex.
4 — Antelope.
5 — Gazelle.
6 — Lion.
7 — Herd of dromedaries.
These carvings differ considerably from the Neolithic ones on the same rocks in style, finish and artistic level (Redrawn after Rothert, 1938).
For comparison later Arab rock carvings are given:
8 — Camel-rider and ibex from Wadi Mukatteb in Sinai (Arconati, 1872).
9 — Camels and rider from Wadi Zelaka by the late Major Kitchener (E. Hull, 1885).

9. The Primaeval Landscapes of the Middle East at the Dawn of History. The fertile crescent of the steppe was the centre of early agriculture and settlement, extended between deserts and forests, both of which were unfavourable to primitive man (Redrawn from Gradmann).

10. The Development of Letters from Pictures of Animals.

a. In Mesopotamia
   A — Bird (issuru).
   B — Fish (nunu).
   C. — Ass (imeru).
   D. — Ox (alpu) (from Chiera).
b. Ancient Cretan Pictographs: bird, bull, starfish, (from Dierenberg).
c. Hittite Royal Inscription. Animal heads which cannot so far be read. The small inset, below at right shows how these animal heads appear in the context. (after Lindl, 1903 p. 32).
d. Letters from the Egyptian Alphabet derived from pictorial hieroglyphs. From left to right: *a, w, f, m* and *ḏ* (From Rowe, 1936, II).
e. Old Egyptian Pictographs for flying (*p3*) and finding (*gm*) (from Dierenberg).

11. SARCOPHAGI OF MUMMIFIED SHREWS FROM EGYPT.

> 1 — The mummified body of *Crocidura religionis,* which was first described from mummies and was discovered still alive in Egypt only many decades later.
> 2 — Sarcophagus of *Crocidura religionis.*
> 3 — Sarcophagus of *Crocidura olivieri.*

The mummies were first treated with tar, then wrapped in small pieces of linen and laid in a sarcophagus modelled from the wood of the sycamore fig tree. The animal itself is carved on the upper surface. Compare the tiny size of *Crocidura religionis* with the great *C. olivieri,* both natural size. (From LORTET and GAILLARD).

12. MAMMALS FROM ANCIENT EGYPTIAN MONUMENTS.

> 1, 2 — *Bos primigenius.*
> 3 — *Ammotragus lervia.*
> 4 — *Dama dama schaeferi.*
> 5 — *Addax nasomaculatus.*
> 6 — *Alcelaphus buselaphus.*
> 7 — *Gazella soemmeringi.*
> 8 — *Cercopithecus pyrrhonotus.*
> 9 — *Papio babuin.*
> 10 — *Sus scropha fera.*
> 11 — Lion devouring man.
> 12 — *Oryx algazal* attacked by greyhound.
> 13 — Above *Lycaon pictus,* below slender hounds.
> 14, 15 — *Lepus aegyptiacus.*
> 16 — Ancient hieroglyph of giraffe.
> 17 — Giraffe as tribute from southern countries in a later period.
> 18 — Elephant hieroglyph.
> 19 — Hippo.
> 20 — Leopard hieroglyph.
> 21 — *Erinaceus auritus.*
> 22 — *Hyaena hyaena.*
> 23 — Rat.
> 24 — Ichneumon

(Mainly redrawn from PATTON, 1925).

13. BIRDS FROM ANCIENT EGYPTIAN MONUMENTS.

> 1 — Little grebe.
> 2 — Avocet.
> 3 — Green plover.
> 4 — Captive cranes being crammed (this bird was often mistaken for the stork).
> 5 — Demoiselle cranes (*Anthropoides virgo*).
> 6 — *Lynch.*
> 7 — Barn owl.
> 8 — *Anas penelope.*
> 9 — *Balaeniceps rex.*
> 10 — Herons in nest.

11 — Mallard in flight (*Anas platyryncha*).
12 — Swan.
13 — Pelican.
14 — Diving pied kingfisher.
15 — Saddle stork (*Ephippiorhynchus senegalensis*).
16 — Bennu-bird or phoenix.
17 — *Corvus ruficollis*.
18 — *Gyps fulvus*.
19 — *Anser albifrons*.
20 — *Anser anser*.
21 — *Alopochen aegyptiaca*.
22 — *Branta ruficollis*.
23 — *Larus* (*marinus*).
24 — *Falco tinnunculus*.
25 — *Falco peregrinoides*.
26 — *Neophron pernopterus*.
27 — Marabu.
1-14 after MOREAU, 15 from HILZHEIMER, 16-27 after WILKINSON and KELLER.

MARINE ANIMALS

14,1. *Carcinas maenas*.
14,2. The spiny lobster *Palinurus vulgaris* (After BREHM).
15,1. Pearl shell *Meleagrinus meleagris*.
15,2. Red coral *Corallium rubrum* (After BREHM).

16. ASSYRIAN LION HUNT FROM TIL BARSIB (Tell Ahmar). Coloured mural painting from bath-room of the Royal palace of TIGLATHPILEZER III (about 735 B.C.; From F. THUREAU-DANGIN).

17. ANCIENT MESOPOTAMIAN ART: Above at left: stag hunt with nets; at right: wild sow and young pigs leaving reed thicket. Following below at left: hind chased by dogs; duck weight; ravens, vultures and eagles feeding upon human carcasses on a battlefield. At right: Landscape showing part of the walls of a besieged city, with fishes in the river and with Assyrian soldiers busy cutting trees with birds' nests. (From LAYARD).

18. ANIMALS ON CYLINDER SEALS FROM MESOPOTAMIA, I.

1 — A lion attracted by an ox is attacked by the hunter as it attacks (500).
2 — Ibex hunted by dog and horseman (517).
3 — Rider spearing a fallow-deer stag (521).
4 — Rider spearing a boar (524).
5 — Spearing fish from a boat (525).
6 — A frieze of mountain sheep (544).
7 — Frieze of scorpions (549).
8 — A frieze of fish (552).
9 — Mountain sheep, wild goat and fallow-deer stag (556).
The figures in brackets refer to O. WEBER, 1920, from which the animals have been redrawn.

19. Animals on Cylinder Seals from Mesopotamia, II.

1 — Gazelles on either side of a plant (563).
2 — Frieze with swimming and flying swans (566).
3 — Lion killing a fallow-deer stag, with eagle (327).
4, 5 — Winged genius with ostriches. In the upper seal the genius is preparing to kill a bird with a knife, in the lower one he is strangling two birds (340, 341).
6 — Lion attacking aurochs and fallow-deer (231).
7 — The dragon (snake) Tihamat is killed by Marduk (347).
8 — Leopard figurine from Warka (5).
9 — Two entwined serpents, one holding a tortoise (106).
10 — The tortoise *Trionyx euphratica* (95).
No. 1-7 as above from O. Weber, no. 8-10 from Van Buren, 1939.

20,1. Fragments from the Ḫar-ra = *Ḫubullu*.

20,2. Locust Prayer in Enamel from Ashur. An Assyrian noble standing before the god Ashur with all his attributes either prays for protection or renders thanks for protection granted against locusts, one of which is drawn above the head of the noble.
(From Bodenheimer).

21,1. Animal Scenes from Ancient Egyptian Mural Paintings, I.

1 — Bird hunt in a papyrus swamp with a decoy bird (a small stick is thrown at the bird).
2 — Various types of bird traps.
3 — The bennu-bird or phoenix of the Egyptians.
4 — Libyan tribute: an ostrich with its eggs and its tail plumes.
5 — Bird scene in Nile swamp.

21,2. Animal Scenes from Ancient Egyptian Mural Paintings, II.

A — Hunting a hippopotamus with harpoons.
B — Southern tribute including ivory, furs, a baboon and a monkey.
C — Captive gazelles from Beni Hassan.
D — Gazelle hind caught in trap. This animal is usually, but without any justification, described as a hyaena.
From Wilkinson.

22. Fishing and Bird Hunting in Ancient Egypt.

A — Man (11) spearing *Tilapia nilotica*. Another man (1), holding a decoy bird, throws a short stick at the birds inhabiting a papyrus swamp. Jungle cat in boat and mongoose (7) preying upon the birds. Dragon flies and moths (9, 10) are also represented.
B — Fishermen catching Nile-fish. These have been identified with the help of the monograph by Gaillard: 1 — *Tilapia nilotica*, 2 — *Mormyrus niloticus*, the oxyrhynchus fish, 3 — *Citharinus latus*, 4 — *Synodontis batensoda*, 5 — *Tetrodon fahaka*, 6 — *Clarias anguillaris*, 7 — ?*Petrocephalus bane*, 8 — ?*Lates niloticus*, 9 — ?*Barbus bynni*, 10 — ?*Labeo niloticus*.
C — Another fishing scene.
After Wilkinson.

23. PAINTED WALL FROM TELEILAT GHASSUL.

Man worshipping enormous ox.
(After VINCENT).

24. VARIOUS ANIMAL FINDS FROM TELEILAT GHASSUL.

1, 2 — Clay figurines of dogs.
3, 4 — Potsherds with dark red animal figures: 3 — gazelle and a water bird, 4 — a
      large bird.
5, 6 — Primitive mammal figures produced by impression of a series of points into the
      wet material (pointillation).
7 — Snake moulded on a jar.
8-10 — Ornamental objects made of mother of pearl.
11 — Shell of a *Leguminaia*, a mollusc living only in the coastal rivers near Jaffa.
12-15 — Various objects made from animal bones.
(The objects in both figures from Teleilat Ghassul have been drawn by kind permission
of the Most Rev. Father FERNANDES, the Prior of the Pontifical Biblical Institute and
Museum at Jerusalem.)

25. ANIMALS IN THE ART OF RAS SHAMRA.

1 — Gold-encrusted bronze hawk (Hyksos influence: about 1600 B.C.).
2 — Cuttle-fish on rhyton (Mycenaean influence; about 1450 B.C.);
3 — Scene from gold cup; Lion attacking ?ibex with vulture above (Mixed Mycenaean,
      Egyptian and Syrian style, typical for Ras Shamra about 1400 B.C.).
After SCHAEFFER.

26. HUNTING SCENE ON GOLD CUP FROM RAS SHAMRA.

After CONTENEAU.

27. ANIMAL FIGURES FROM TELL HALAF, I.

1 — Archer hunting wild bull. Please note that a thick line separates the front of the
      bull from the horn. This clearly indicates that the horn is intended to rise from
      the far side, and certainly not from the middle of the forehead.
2 — Statue of a giant eagle. Observe the disproportionately big head.
1 and 2 belong to the old objects of the temple which are dated before 2000 B.C.
3 — Orthostate depicting bull hunt from chariot. Whereas the object no. 1 was modelled
      in hard basalt, the orthostates are mainly made of soft lime-stone. Here the two
      horns of the bull are clearly represented.

28. ANIMAL FIGURES FROM TELL HALAF, II.

Big Orthostate with Animal Choir. Explanation in text, p. 161.
After VON OPPENHEIM.

29. ANIMAL FIGURES ON ORTHOSTATES OF THE TEMPLE AT TELL HALAF (about 11th century
B.C.).

1 — Camel-rider.
2 — Man on foot (apparently Gilgamesh) killing a lion with a sword whilst the lion
      bites into the right arm of the hero.
3 — Leopard.

4 — Ostrich; above partridge (certainly not falcon, but possibly domestic fowl).
5 — Wild goose.
6 — Wild bull killing a lioness.
7 — Wild boar.
8 — Lion killing a fallow-deer stag.
9 — Man with fishing-rod.
10 — Boat on river with fish.
After VON OPPENHEIM and objects in the National Museum at Aleppo.

30. A GROUP OF AAMU under sheikh Abeshu bring an ibex, a gazelle, and kohl to the pharaoh. The asses as only mode of transport, the clothing, the musical instruments, etc. are of interest. From a tomb painting of the 19th century B.C. at Beni Hassan.

31. VARIOUS ANIMALS IN EGYPTIAN MURAL PAINTINGS:

A — Tribute from Syria-Palestine with an Asiatic elephant, ivory, a Syrian bear and horses. From the tomb of REKHMERA.
B — Syrian bears on potsherds from the tomb of SAHEW-RA (after GRESSMANN).
C — Some animals from THUTMOSIS III's temple at Karnak: 1 — Oxen with head-decoration; 2 — calf of no. 1; 3 — hornless cattle; 4 — hind of gazelle; 5 — uraeus snake; 6 — copulating locusts.
D — Nile crocodile from the mastaba of Gemnikai (VON BISSING and WEIGAND, 1905).
E — Syrian cattle imported into Egypt. From painting at el-Bershah (ROWE).

32. THE BIRDS FROM THE BOTANICAL GARDEN IN THE TEMPLE OF THUTMOSIS III AT KARNAK:

1 — *Columbalivia.*
2 — Sandpiper.
3 — *Ammoperdix heyi.*
4 — Accipitrid bird.
5 — Desert raven or jackdaw.
6 — Gull.
7 — Spurred plover.
8 — *Alectoris graeca.*
9 — Cormorant (not a fregat bird, as HILZHEIMER supposes).
10 — Turtle dove.
11 — *Anhinga chantrei.*
12 — *Egretta alba.*
13 — Rock-dove.
14 — Bean-goose.
15 — Great spotted cuckoo.
16 — (Swallow or) cuckoo.
17 — Crane.
18 — Swimming duck.
19 — *Casarca.*
20 — Plover.
21 — Goose.
22 — Houbara.
23 — Glossy ibis.
24 — Kestrel.

33. Animals on early Bronze Pottery from Palestine (Tell Ajjul).

Cattle, various birds and fishes. Among the birds eagle, raven and dove can be identified, among the fishes—with doubt—an anchovy, a Triglid, a makerel and a Cangrid (Dr Lisser det.). The two birds of the upper row belong to an older period since only the outlines are drawn and the interior is filled with dots or stripes.
From Heurtly by kind permission of the Department of Antiquities, Jerusalem.

34. Goats eating Leaves. On a potsherd from Gezer (from Macalister).

35. Domestic Animals from Gezer, I.

1-5 — Horns of domestic cattle in five periods of Gezer: 1 — from the Pre-Semitic and the first Semitic period; 2 — from the second; 3 — from the third; 4 — from the fourth Semitic period; and 5 — from the Hellenistic strata.
6 — Torso of zebu figurine.
7 — Bull figurine.
8-9 — Cattle with ridges along the horns.
10 — Ox bearing yoke.
11 — Head of camel.
12 — A double-cat amulet.
13-16 — Various horse trappings.
17 — Donkey trappings.
18 — Rider on horse.
19 — Engraved horse and rider from a votive altar.
20 — Bronze horse-bit.
21 — Galloping horse.
22 — Ram's head.
23 — Goat's head.
24 — Sheep's head.
25 — Slab of limestone with graffito of a man with two goats.
26 — Pig or bear?
27 — Ass with load or camel with hump.
28 — Camel's head.
29 — Camel pendant from the Bronze period.
From Macalister, 1912.

36. Domestic Animals from Gezer, II.

1 — Potsherd with ostrich.
2 — Pottery duck with feathers inserted.
3 — Head of figurine of goose or swan.
4 — Potsherd with swimming swan.
5 — Graffito of arthropod from a bowl.
6-7 — Zoomorphic vessels.
8 — Bird figurine.
9 — Fish figurine from tomb.
10 — Crude elephant(?) figurine.
11 — Stag figurine.

12 — Lion's head from the Byzantine period.
13 — Ivory inlays in the form of birds.
14-15 — Potsherd with snakes.
16-17 — Fish-hooks.
18-21 — Graffiti from the Thamudic period on cave walls. These graffiti were originally believed to be the work an of early troglodyte population. No. 19 was regarded by MACALISTER as a millipede (*Spirostreptus*), but the evidence is too slight to permit this identification.
From MACALISTER, 1912.

37. DOMESTIC ANIMALS FROM GEZER, III.

1 — Brazen serpent.
2 — Bone needles.
3 — Bone needle case with contents.
4 — Ivory pin.
5 — Bone support for chains of beads.
6 — Various bone objects.
7 — Metacarpal of a goat as amulet.
8 — Spindle whorl cut from human femur-head.
9 — Clay tablet with figures of the zodiac.
10 — Amulets made from boar tusks.
11 — Coral amulet.
12-16 — Animals on early Semitic pottery.
12-14 — Animals and birds.
15 — Octopus.
16 — Small birds and shrub.
17-18 — Animal scenes on Hellenistic votive altar: Fight of man and lion, man killing an animal, stag and hind, lion attacking ass.
From MACALISTER, 1912.

38. ANIMALS FROM TA'ANNEK.

1 — Rider on camel in clay.
2 — Head of bull.
3 — Potsherd with ibex.
4 — Seal with gazelles flanking a tree.
5 — ?Jackal as handle of a jar.
6 — Hellenistic lamp with eagle, hare and lion.
7 — Boy killing serpent from the left wall of the incense altar (no. 10).
8 — Lion's head.
9 — Frontal view of amulet with scorpion.
10 — Large incense altar with lions, sphinxes with human heads, below: tree with two ibexes.
After E. SELLIN 1904, 1905

39. IVORY VASE FROM TELL DUWEIR. Fighting lions and bulls; Eagle with outstretched wings. Late Bronze II. (See also Plate XVIII).

40. MEGIDDO IVORIES AND OTHER ANIMAL REMAINS.

    1 — Ivory jar lid with horned animals (probably stylized gazelles).
    2 — Disk with ibex (piece of a game).
    3 — Ivory bull's head.
    4 — Horn-shaped object, probably from a boar's tusk. Inside hollow; walls 3 mm thick.
    5 — Fragments of an ivory fish-shaped plate, perhaps for ointment.
    6 — Pottery figurine of a sheep with a fat tail.
    7 — Animals on a jar.
    8-10 — View and cross-section of horns of some domestic animals.
    8 — *Bos cf. longifrons.*
    9 — *Capra hircus mambrica.*
    10 — *Ovis sp.*
    After GUY, ENGLING and BATE.

41. IVORIES FROM MEGIDDO.

    1 — Men and geese.
    2 — War chariots in battle.
    3 — Three surfaces of a quadrangular ivory bar, showing hunter of ibexes and hinds, bulls fighting with lions, and lions and deer.
    4 — Double comb with lion beneath trees.
    5 — Comb with dog attacking ibex.
    Redrawn from the reconstructions of G. G. LOUD.

42. RECONSTRUCTION OF THE WALLS, THE ROYAL PALACE AND THE ROYAL STABLES OF KING SOLOMON AT MEGIDDO. All the small buildings in the background are stables. Redrawn after OLMSTEAD.

43. ANIMALS FROM MEGIDDO.

    1 — Locust seal. Griffin (symbol of Royal strength) over a locust (symbol of multitude and weakness). After STAPLES, 1931.
    2, 3 — Stylized animals (impressions of cylinder seals on pottery).
    4 — Baboon?
    5 — Stag of red deer.
    6 — Ibex. After ENGBERG & SHIPTON, 1934.
    7 — Egyptian locust pendants, probably amulets against locust plagues. Such amulets, usually made of glass, are found in Egypt in all strata and also occur in Palestine. From FLINDERS PETRIE, 1914.

44. IVORY FROM SAMARIA, Grazing fallow-deer.

    After CROWFOOT, 1938.

45. SACRIFICIAL VESSELS FROM SOLOMON'S TEMPLE.

    1 — Molten Sea.
    2 — Brass vase on wheels.
    3 — Seven-armed candelabrum.
    Partly after BENZINGER.

46. JONAH ENTERING AND LEAVING THE WHALE'S MOUTH. The clothing and the hairs of the prophet have been eaten away by the digestive juices of the whale. (From a manuscript of the 14th century; SCHMIDT 1907.) Below: JONAH sitting in the stomach of the whale. From the old Byzantinian Chludoff psalter at Moscow.

47. SOME PALESTINIAN SEALS.

1 — A seal of the Roman period showing Dionysus milking a goat. This goat is *Capra pseudo-falconeri* with screwed horns, which is found also on Syrian miniatures of the Byzantine period. On Roman gems of the same subject *Capra aegagrus* with simply curved horns is always depicted.

2 — Israelite seal with lion, ibex, and scorpion.

3 — Israelite seal of stone curlew.

Mr. R. JONAS, Jerusalem, kindly permitted reproduction of these seals from his private collection.

48. A. — Mesopotamian fish-god. The Philistine Dagon is assumed to have been often represented in a similar way.

B — Atergatis.

C — Camel-rider from southern tells.

From BLISS and MACALISTER.

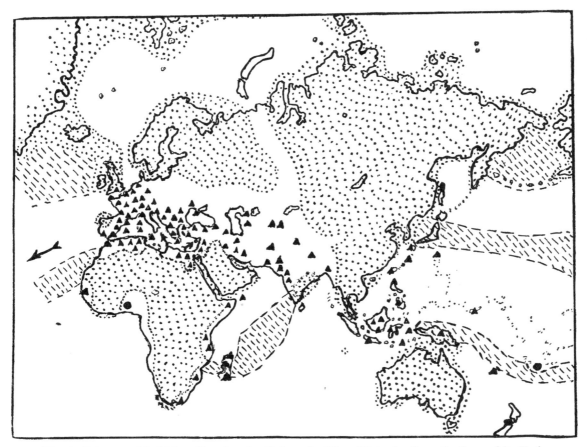

Fig. 1. Palaeographical Maps Showing the Tethys, the Rise of Palestine from the Sea and its Early
Continental Connections. 1. Cretaceous to Oligocenous Continents.
See p. 15.

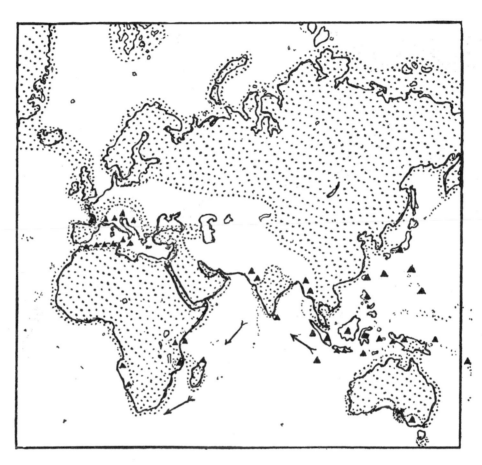

Fig. 1. Palaeographical Maps Showing the Tethys, the Rise of Palestine from the Sea
and its Early Continental Connections. 2. Upper Oligocene to Later Miocene Continents.
See p. 15.

Fig. 2. Savannah Landscape of Attica in the Lower Pliocene.
See p. 15.

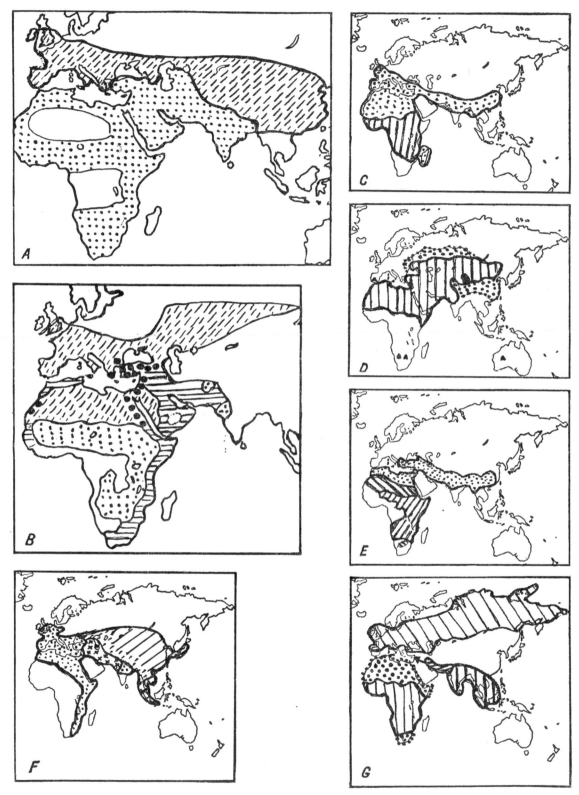

Fig. 3. Palaeographic Distribution of Some Animals. I.
See p. 16ff.

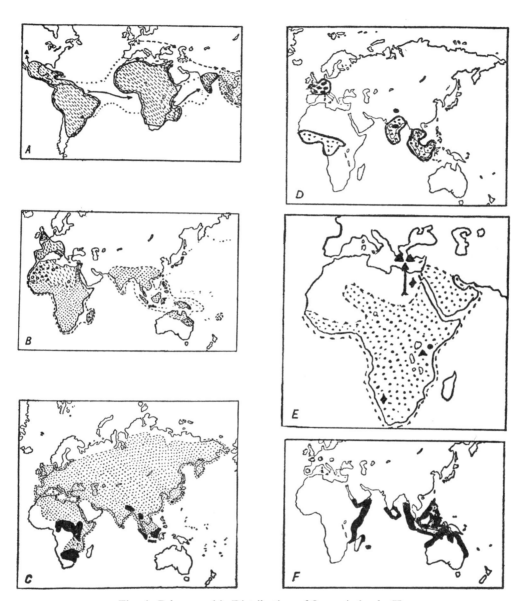

Fig. 4. Palaeographic Distribution of Some Animals. II.
See p. 16ff.

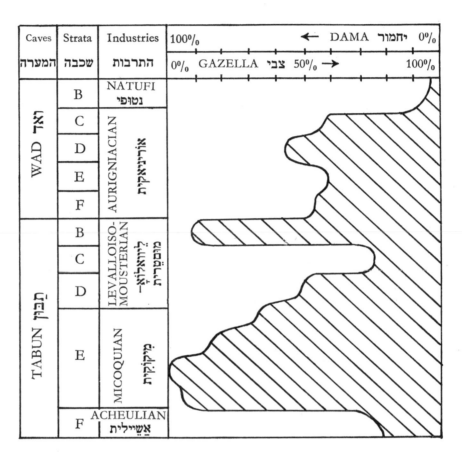

Caves המערה	Strata שכבה	Industries התרבות					

Fig. 5. The Sequence of Cave-Strata and Stone-Industries in the Mt. Carmel.
See p. 19ff.

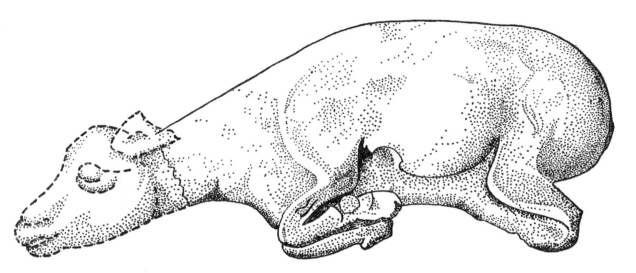

Fig. 6. Natufian Gazelle Sculpture.
See p. 22.

Fig. 7. Neolithic Rock Carvings from Kilwa.
See p. 33ff.

Fig. 8. Nabathaean Rock Carvings from Kilwa.
See p. 35.

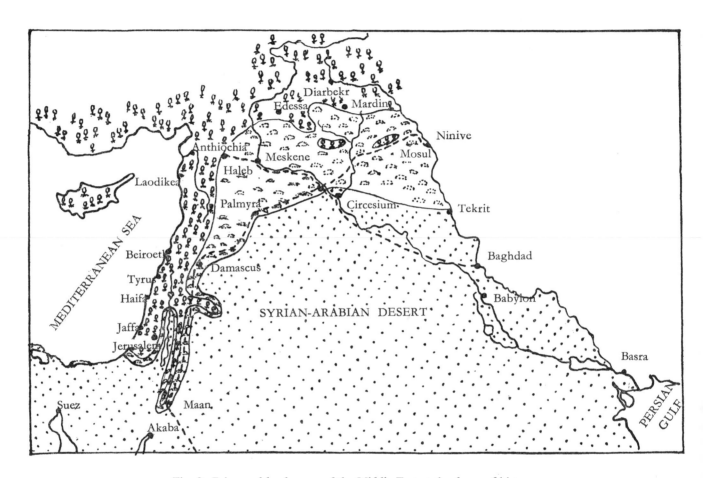

Fig. 9. Primaeval landscapes of the Middle East at the dawn of history.
See p. 35ff.

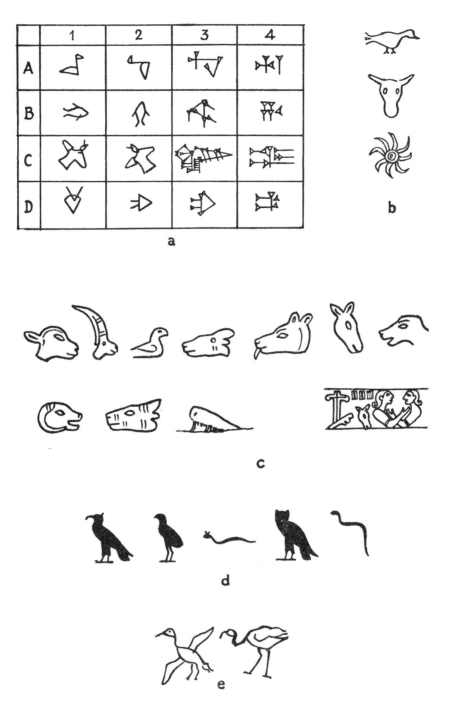

Fig. 10. The Development of Letters from Pictorial Animals.

Fig. 11. Sarcophagi of Mummified Shrews from Egypt.
See p. 41f.

Fig. 12. Mammals from Ancient Egyptian Monuments.
See p. 123.

Fig. 13. Birds from Ancient Egyptian Monuments.
See p. 123ff.

Fig. **14,1**. Marine Animals I. *Carcinas Maenas*.
See p. 82 ff.

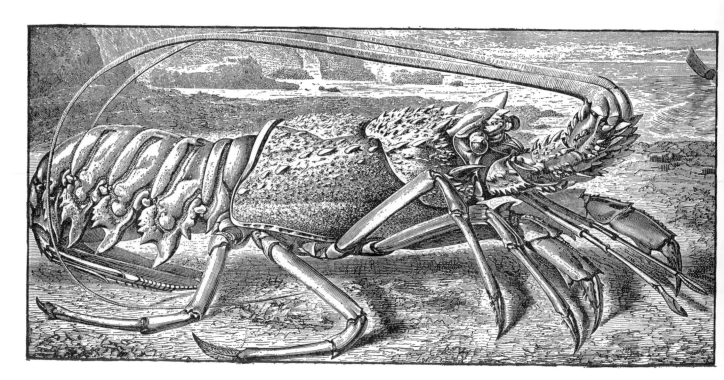

Fig. 14,2. Marine Animals II. *Palinurus Vulgaris*.
See p. 82 ff.

Fig. 15,1. Marine Animals. III. *Meleagrinus Meleagris*.
See p. 82 ff.

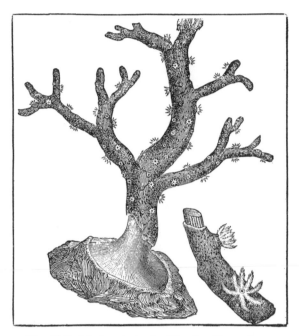

Fig. 15,2. Marine Animals. IV. *Corallium rubrum*.
See p. 82 ff.

Fig. 16. Assyrian Lion Hunt from Til Barsib.
See p. 100.

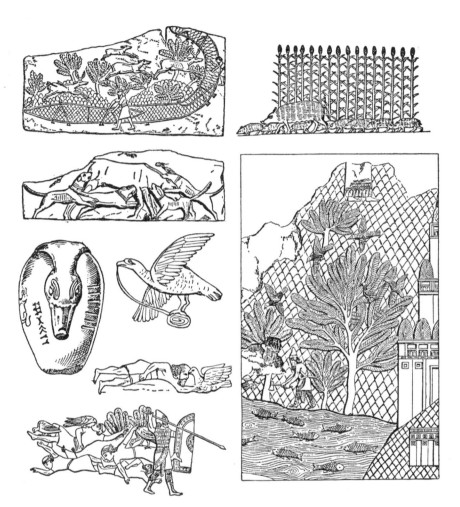

Fig. 17. Ancient Mesopotamian Art.

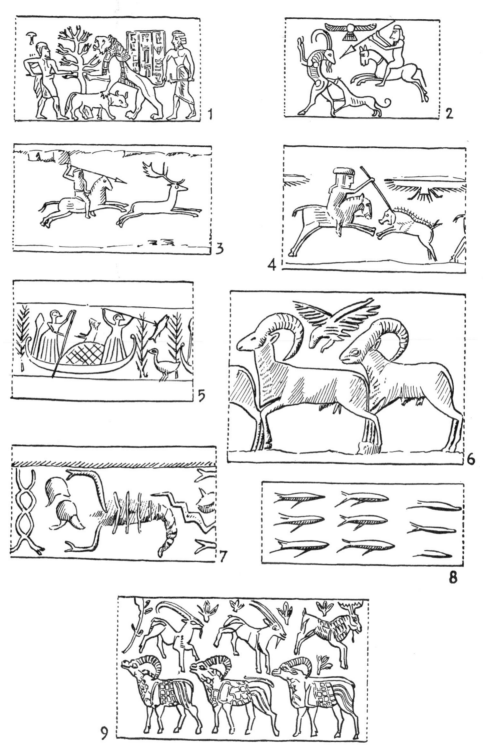

Fig. 18. Animals on Cylinder Seals from Mesopotamia I.
See p. 100ff.

Fig. 19. Animals on Cylindric Seals from Mesopotamia II.
See p. 100ff.

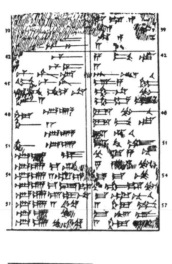

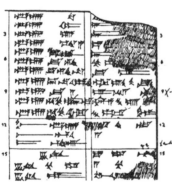

Fig. 20,1. Fragments from Ḫar-ra =
Ḫubullu.
See ch. 2.24.

Fig. 20,2. Locust Prayer in Enamel from
Ashur.
See p. 105.

Fig. 21,1. Animal Scenes from Ancient Egyptian Mural Paintings. I.

Fig. 21,2. Animal Scenes from Ancient Egyptian Mural Paintings. II.

Fig. 22. Fishing and Bird Hunting in Ancient Egypt.

Fig. 23. Painted wall from Teleilat Ghassul.
See p. 154.

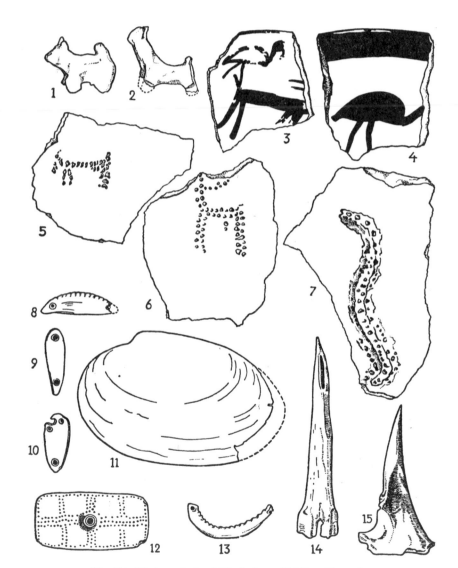

Fig. 24. Various Animal Finds from Teleilat Ghassul.
See p. 154.

Fig. 25. Animals in the Art of Ras Shamra.
See p. 156.

Fig. 26. Hunting Scene on Gold Cup.
See p. 156.

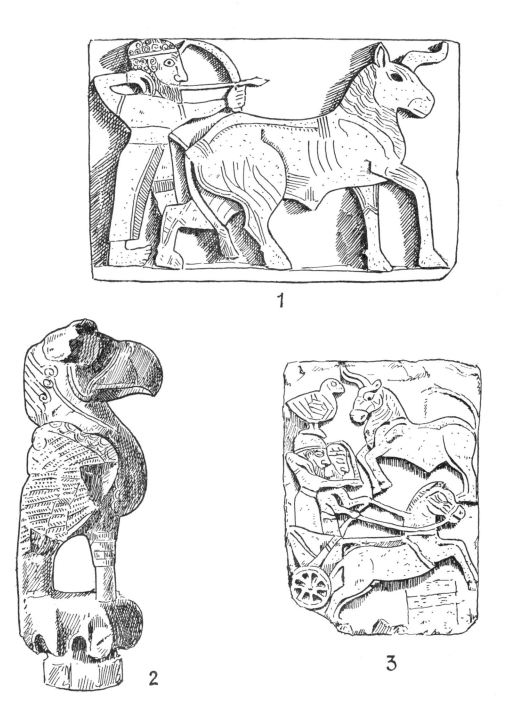

Fig. 27. Animal Figures from Tell Halaf. I.
See p. 160.

Fig. 28. Animal Figures from Tell Halaf. II.
See p. 161.

Fig. 29. Animal Figures on Orthostates of the Temple of Tell Halaf.
See p. 160f.

Fig. 30. A Group of Aamu Bringing Tribute to the Pharaoh.
See p. 161f.

Fig. 31. Various Animals in Egyptian Mural Paintings.
See p. 164 and 168.

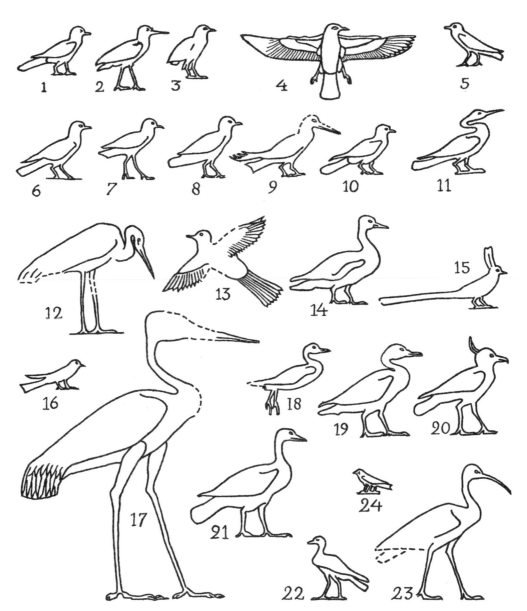

Fig. 32. The Birds from the Botanical Garden in the Temple of Thutmosis III at Karnak.
See p. 168.

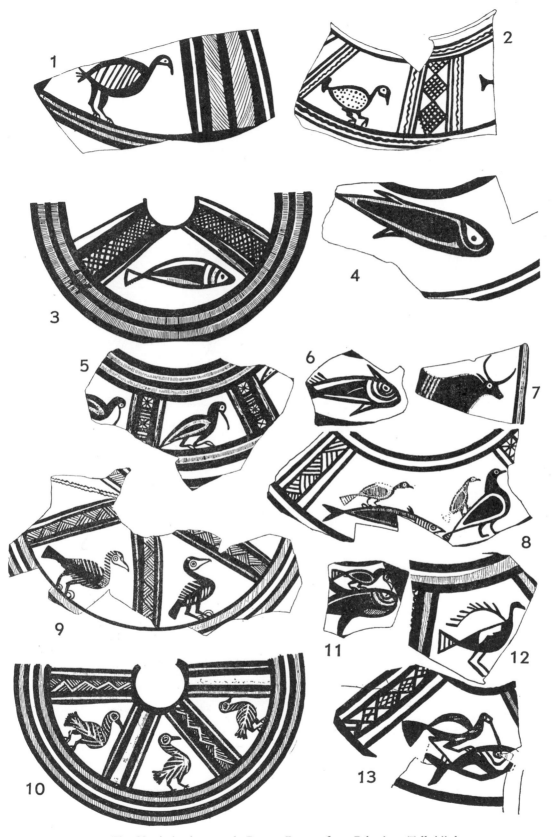

Fig. 33. Animals on early Bronze Pottery from Palestine. Tell Ajjul.

Fig. 34. Goats eating leaves.
(Potsherd from Gezer)

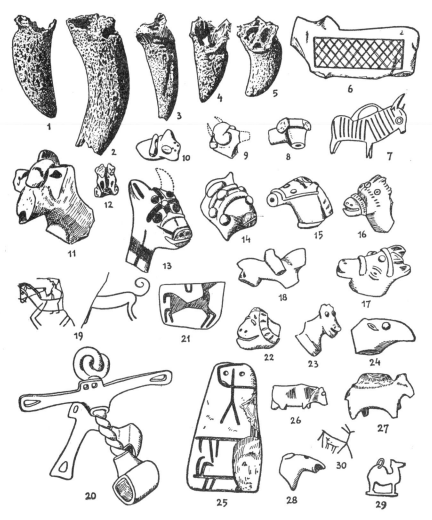

Fig. 35. Domestic Animals at Gezer. I.
See p. 178f.

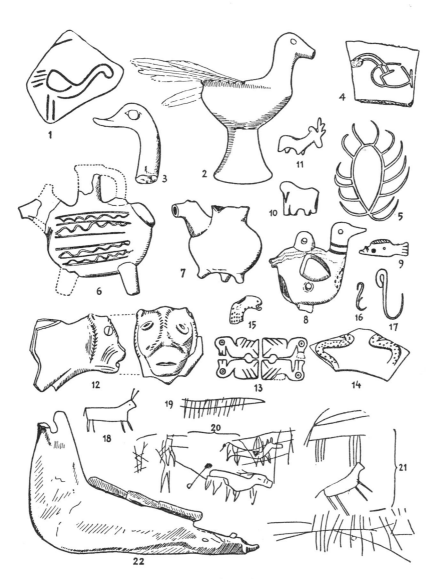

Fig. 36. Domestic Animals at Gezer. II.
See p. 179.

Fig. 37. Domestic Animals from Gezer. III.
See p. 179ff.

Fig. 38. Animals from Ta'annek.
See pp. 179 and 183.

Fig. 39. Ivory vase. Tell Duweir.

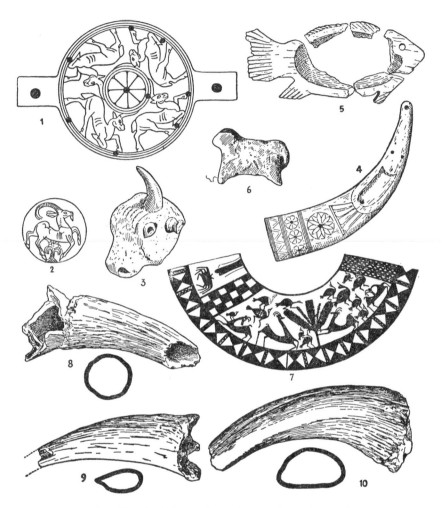

Fig. 40. Megiddo Ivories and other Animal Remains.
See p. 187.

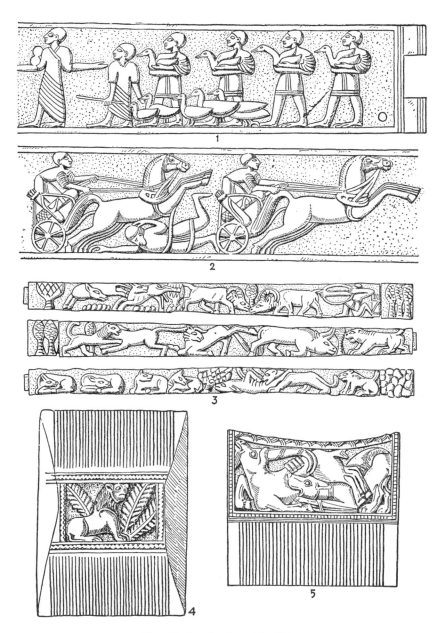

Fig. 41. Ivories from Megiddo.
See p. 188ff.

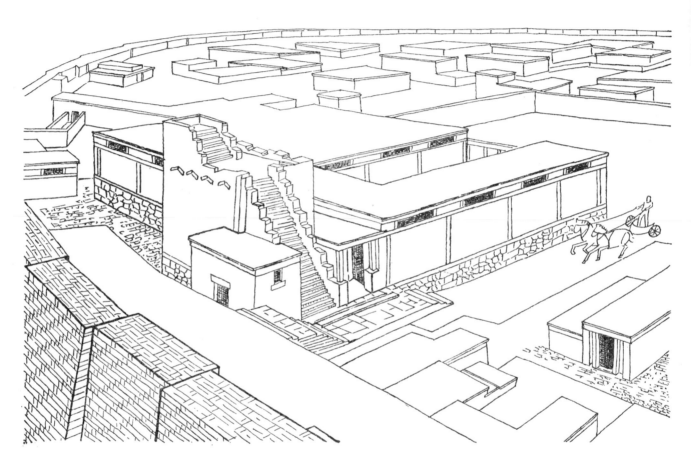

Fig. 42. Reconstruction at Megiddo.
See p. 188ff.

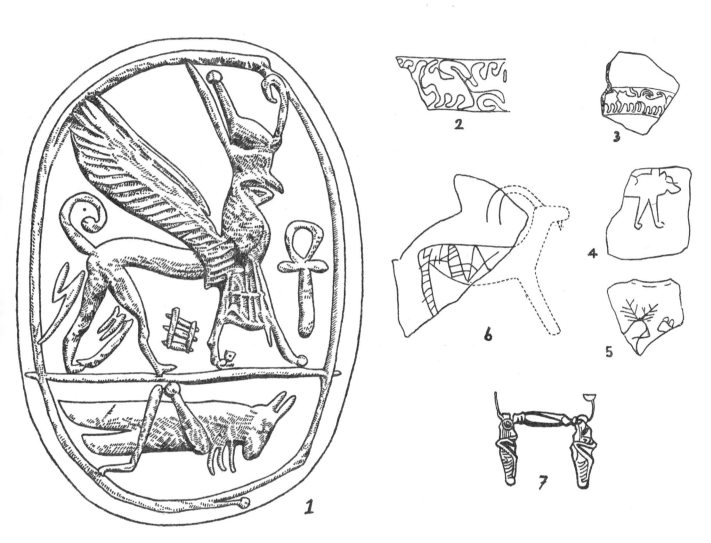

Fig. 43. Animals from Megiddo.

Fig. 44. Ivory from Samaria.

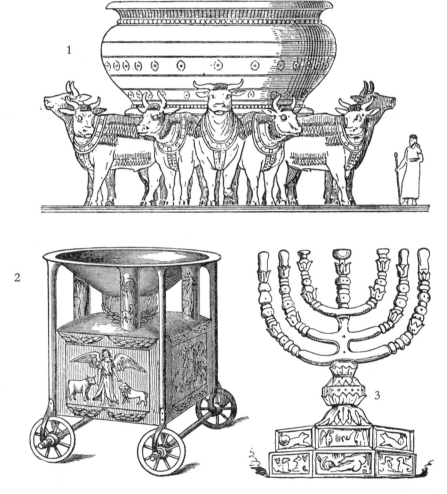

Fig. 45. Sacrificial Vessels from Solomon's Temple.
See p. 176.

Fig. 46. Jonah Entering and Leaving the Whale's Mouth.
See p. 202.

1   2   3

Fig. 47. Some Palestine Seals.

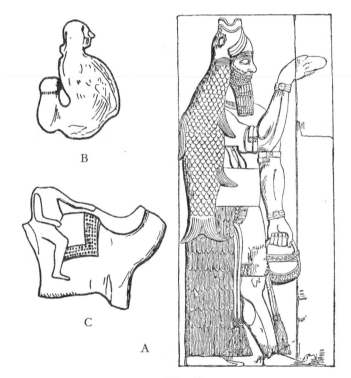

B

C

A

Fig. 48.

PLATES

I. Bones, Teeth, and Horns of Animals of the Palestine Stone Age.

  1, 2 — Canines of *Ursus cf. arctos* from the Upper Palaeolithicum of the caves of Wad and of Zuttiyeh.

  3 — Lower and upper molars of *Dama dama mesopotamica*. Zuttiyeh. Upper Palaeolithicum.

  4 — Fragment of lower jaw of *Hyaena crocuta*. Wad. Upper Palaeolithicum.

  5 — Horn of gazelle from Zuttiyeh. Upper Palaeolithicum.

  6 — *Bos cf. primigenius*. Upper molars. Mugharet es-Sukhul. Upper Palaeolithicum.

  7 — Tusk of *Elephas cf. trogantherium*. Jisr Banat Yaqub. Lower Palaeolithicum.

  8-12 — Horns of Natufian gazelles: 8 Kebara, 9 Wad B, 19-12 Mugharet es-Zuttiyeh.

II. Bone Tools from the Stone Age.

  1 — Six harpoons with 1 to 5 hooks on one side made from polished bones. Mugharet el-Kebara. Lower Natufian.

  2 — Four fish-hooks of polished bone. As 1.

  3 — Two finely pointed harpoons from the fin spines of a percomorph fish. As 1.

  4 — Needles made from polished articulate bones. As 1.

  5 — Awl made from antler of roe-deer. Mugharet el-Wad. Natufian.

  6 — Pierced shells, mainly *Pectunculus* and *Dentalium* used as ornament. Mugharet el Kebara. Natufian.

  7 — Skin rubber made from antler of the fallow-deer. Wad B. Natufian.

  8, 10, 11 — Bone awls or points from Wadi Mughara. Mesolithicum.

  9 — Awl. Wad E. Upper Palaeolithicum.

III. Art in the Palestine Stone Age.

  1 — Necklace of 25 separately worked twin pendants of polished bones with dentalium shells strung between them. Wad. Upper Palaeolithicum.

  2 — Head of bovine animal carved in bone as top part of a sickle shaft. Mugharet el-Kebara. Mesolithicum.

  3, 4 — Grooved sickle-blade shafts with goat's head carved in bone. As 2.

  5, 6 — Head of bovine animal carved in bone, from sickle shaft. Mugharet el Kebara. Mesolithicum.

IV. Photographs of the Neolithic Ibex Carvings at Kilwa. From Glueck.

V. Animal Seals from the Mohenjo Daro Civilisation of the Indus Valley (2500 B.C.). Above: Aurochs bull (not unicorn) and zebu bull. Middle: Short-horned, perhaps arni bull, tiger and Indian elephant. Below: Indian rhinoceros, garial

(Ganges crocodile), and a bull-man fighting a tiger (The big "horns" above the tiger's head are not ears, but belong to the inscription. The animal is a typical tiger and not a monster, as assumed; From Atlantis 1932 no. X).

VI. A. Aurochs (*Bos primigenius*) drawn from life about 150 years ago by a Polish artist.
    B. Assyrian illustration of the hunting of aurochs with nets. (Both after HILZHEIMER).

VII. A. The Nubian wild ass (*Asinus nubianus*), the ancestor of the domestic ass.
    B. The Syrian onager (*Asinus hemihippus*). (Both from MILNE EDWARDS).

VIII. A. The asp or uraeus-snake (*Naja haje*; from the *Déscription de l'Egypte*).
    B. The Palestine Viper (*Vipera palaestinae*; from TRISTRAM).

IX. ASSYRIAN MONUMENTS:

    A. Model of a liver with indication of the various parts of importance for sacral omens. Such tablets served as teaching models in the seminaries.
    B. A boundary stone from Ritti-Marduk showing signs of the zodiac (scorpion and archer), snakes, hedgehog, eagle and domestic animals.
    (From publications of the British Museum).

X. FRESHWATER IDYL FROM MARSHES OF C. IRAK with fishes, snails and crabs amongst the reeds (Relief from Kujunjik, after LAYARD).

XI. ENEMIES OF ASSYRIA TAKE REFUGE ON SHIPS, WITH SCENES OF MARINE LIFE. Fishes, crabs, sea-stars, turtles and some reptile like forms are represented. (Relief from Kujunjik, after LAYARD).

XII. ANIMALS FROM THE MURAL PAINTINGS OF TELEILAT GHASSUL.

    Above: The bird picture: only head, legs and the forked tail are preserved, all in black.
    Below: A water bird (red and black) from the star picture.

XIII. THE "BOTANICAL GARDEN" ROOM IN THE TEMPLE OF THUTMOSIS III AT KARNAK.

    A. The state of conservation (from CAPART).
    B. Sample sector from the frieze of plants and animals from Retenu (Palestine): Above: gull?, spurred plover, partridge, cormorant?, turtle dove, rock dove, sandpiper, African darter. Middle: goose and peewit. Below: White heron, calf of hornless ox. (From WRESZINSKY).

XIV. BIRDS, HOOPOE, SHRIKES AND REDBREAST IN AN ACACIA TREE (*Aracia arabica*).

    One of the most beautiful animal scenes and compositions from ancient Egypt. From a wall painting in the tomb of Khnumhetep II at Beni Hassan (After DAVIES). Explanation in text, p. 164.

XV. ANIMAL SCULPTURE FROM PALESTINE.

1 — Three "Bambi" fawns of gazelles from Tell Duweir. Bronze.
2 — Ivory bull's head. Megiddo, 1250 B.C.
3 — Ivory bull's head. Jericho. Early Bronze III.
4 — Offering bowl with three lions, seen from the side. Tell Beit Mirsim. Late Bronze.

XVI. SCARAB SEALS OF PALESTINIAN PROVENANCE, AND MANY AMONGST THEM OF LOCAL MANUFACTURE.

1 — Couchant hippopotamus. Tell Ajjul. Hyksos (309).
2 — Ibex with crocodile above. Jericho. Hyksos (312).
3 — Lion jumping on ibex. Tell Ajjul. Hyksos (320).
4 — Lion over crocodile, with uraeus in front. Jericho. Hyksos (319).
5 — Man holding a great shield to hide behind in stalking game (Petrie). Uraeus in front. Beth-Shan. Hyksos (298).
6 — Bull trampling on captive. Tell Ajjul. 18th dynasty (527).
7 — Man holding a gazelle with his right hand and spearing it with his left. Above the gazelle are perhaps two hunting (?) falcons, below it a young gazelle. Megiddo. 19th dynasty (SO. 9).
8 — Seated lion with the tongue hanging out, doubtless dying, as a vulture sits on its back. Tell Fara. Hyksos (324).
9 — Giraffe. Tell Ajjul. 18th dynasty (S. 36).
10 — Crocodile over lion. Tell Jemmeh. Hyksos (318).
11 — Falcon and ? scorpions. Megiddo 15th dynasty (167).
12 — Man or god holding two ostriches. Gezer. 20th dynasty (SO. 14).
13 — Scarabaeus beetle. Megiddo. 13th dynasty (54).
14 — Duck upon serpent, uraeus above. Tell Ajjul. 18th dynasty (576).
15 — Two scorpions head to tail, probably worn as amulet against scorpion stings. Tell Fara. 19th dynasty (738).
16 — Fish. Tell Ajjul. 18th dynasty (597).
17 — Above wounded animal (? lion) with blood pouring out of its mouth. Below at left winged griffin (?), at right ibex. Tell Ajjul. 11th dynasty (S. 2).
18-21 — Various amulets:
18 — Hippopotamus, one of the common Seth-animals. Ain Shems (?; A 33).
19 — Couchant hare. Atlit. 27th dynasty (A 42).
20 — Couchant cat. Beth-Shan. 18th dynasty (A 38).
21 — Frog. Tell Ajjul. (A 45).
The ciphers in brackets indicate the number in A. ROWE (1936).

XVII. HORSE BURIAL FROM A HYKSOS TOMB AT ANCIENT GAZA. (From FLINDERS-PETRIE).

XVIII. ANIMAL FIGURINES FROM THE SOUTHERN TELLS OF PALESTINE.

Above: Bronze horse-bit, with circular cheek plates with sharp teeth. Tell Ajjul. Middle Bronze; Hollow golden fly-amulets with fly-maggot. Tell Ajjul. Late Bronze; Crouching ivory cat. Tell Duweir. Late Bronze; Ivory figurine of crouching calf. Tell Duweir. Late Bronze.

Below: Blackened ivory carvings of men hunting and netting birds and fishes, with bull in an Egyptian papyrus thicket, but of local craftsmanship. Tell Fara. Late Bronze II; Cylindrical ivory vase with fighting lions and bulls, and with an eagle with outstretched wings. Tell Duweir. Late Bronze II. (See also fig. 39).

XIX. Bowl, the interior with horned animals and birds. Ain Shems. Late Bronze.

XX. Lion and Dog Stele from Beth-shan (From Glueck).

XXI. Two Votive Vases with snakes and windows, serving either for the burning of incense or as Adonis gardens. Beth-shan.

XXII. A. Samaria Ivories of the 9th Century B.C.

1, 2 — Carved sitting lions in high relief.
3 — Ivory inlay representing lion fighting bull.

B. Animal Representations from Megiddo.

1 — Carved rectangular box with lions and cherubim in high relief. Megiddo. 1250 B.C.
2 — Head of accipitrine bird in ivory. Megiddo.
3 — Golden finger ring with two ?jackals flanking a Hathor-headed column. Tell Ajjul. Late Bronze.
4 — Cosmetic box in duck-shape. Megiddo. Middle Bronze.
5 — Bone plaque with crouching lion and gazelle flanking a tree. Tell Beit Mirsim. Late Bronze.
6 — Bone plaque with a running fawn. Tell Beit Mirsim. Middle Bronze II.

XXIII. A. Old Egyptian Horus Amulet (from Bodenheimer).

B. Amulet with Hebrew Inscription against the demons of the night with a she-wolf (Tell Arslan 7th century B.C.; from Torczyner).

XXIV. Animal Clay Figurines.

1, 2 — Cow. Jericho Stratum X and XII. Neolithic.
3 — Dog with pointed muzzle and large ears. Jericho Stratum X. Neolithic.
4-6 — Dog. Teleilat Ghassul. Chalcolithic.
7 — Donkey. Megiddo. Early Bronze.
8, 9 — Bull. Cyprus ware found in Palestine. Late Bronze.
10 — Horse and rider. Amman. Iron II.
11 — Incense burner in shape of a pig's head. Beth-Shan. Late Bronze.
12 — Bull vase. Amman. Iron II.
13 — Sheep with fat tail. Megiddo. Middle Bronze.

XXV. The Inhabitants of Destroyed Lachish on their Way to the Galuth in N. Mesopotamia. The cars are drawn by cattle, still very similar to the aurochs, other goods are transported on camels. (From Kujunjik, after Layard).

XXVI. FAMOUS AND INTERESTING ANIMAL SEALS FROM PALESTINE.

1 — Walking lion. Tell Fara. Hyksos.
2 — Locust seal of Megiddo. (See also fig. 43, 1).
3 — Bronze weight from Ascalon in the shape of a tortoise. One eighth shekel: 2,63 gr. 5th century B.C. (From REIFENBERG, 1939 pl. III. A).
4 — Winged uraeus serpent. (From REIFENBERG 1938).
5 — Rooster seal of Tell el-Nesbeh. Early 6th century B.C.
6 — The lion seal of SHEMA, the servant of REHOBEAM. Megiddo.
7 — Rooster seal of SHEMAB, of Palestine provenience, but bought in Cairo. 9th or 8th century B.C. The rooster is the oldest or one of the oldest illustrations of the domestic fowl. (REIFENBERG 1939 pl. XXXIV fig. 5).
8 — Ibex. After REIFENBERG.

XXVII. A. A TABLET CARVED IN GYPSUM (8 × 15 cm) found near Caesarea in the dunes, probably from the last centuries B.C. It begins above at right with a lion and a lioness, turns into a scene of sacrificial animals (sheep, ram, etc.), ending in a sacrificial act. Most interesting is the lowest row, depicting a crocodile hunt with harpoons at the right, the dragging away of a crocodile carcass by oxen at the left. This crocodile tablet is of special interest, as it was found in the neighbourhood of the Crocodile River near Tantura. The script has not yet been deciphered. The circumstances of the find and the uniqueness of the tablet as well as some details of the craftmanship strongly point to its genuineness.

B. A YOUNG BULL IN BRONZE FROM RAS EL-EIN (apparently 5th century B.C.). In accordance with the general tradition it represents the broad-fronted, short-horned cattle of that period, which later was largely replaced by the zebu. We express our sincere thanks to Mr. R. JONAS, Jerusalem, who kindly permitted the reproduction of these unique objects from his private collection.

Plate I

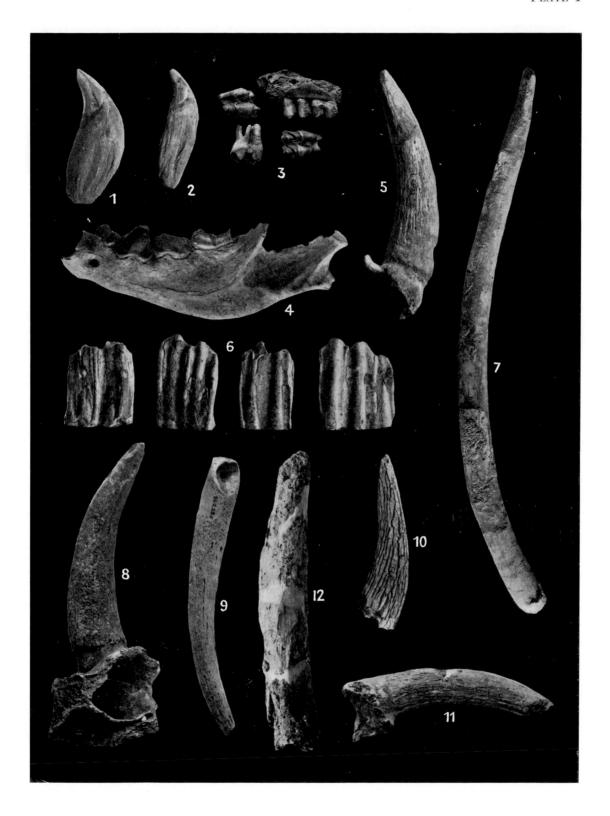

PLATE II

PLATE III

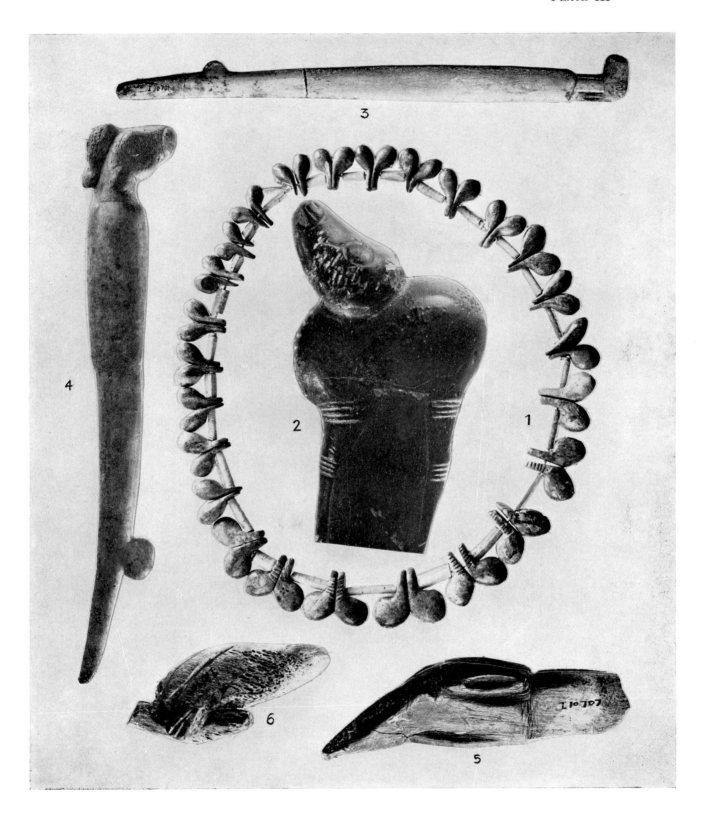

PLATE IV

A.

B.

PLATE V

Plate VI

A.

B.

PLATE VII

A.

B.

PLATE VIII

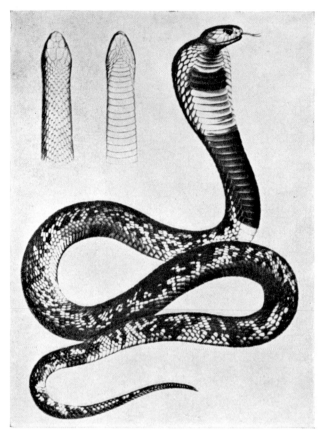

A.

B.

PLATE IX

A.

B.

Plate X

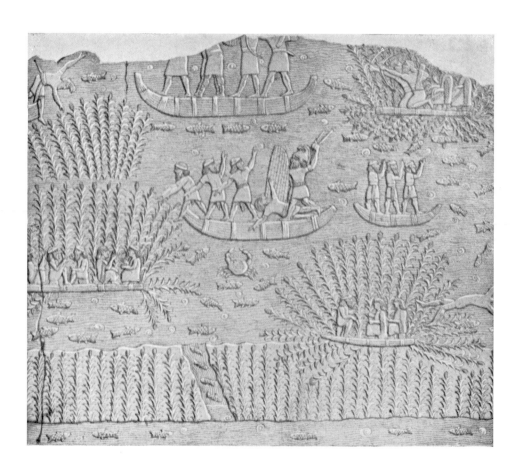

PLATE XI

PLATE XII

A.

B.

PLATE XIII

A.

B.

PLATE XIV

PLATE XV

1.

2.   3.

4.

PLATE XVI

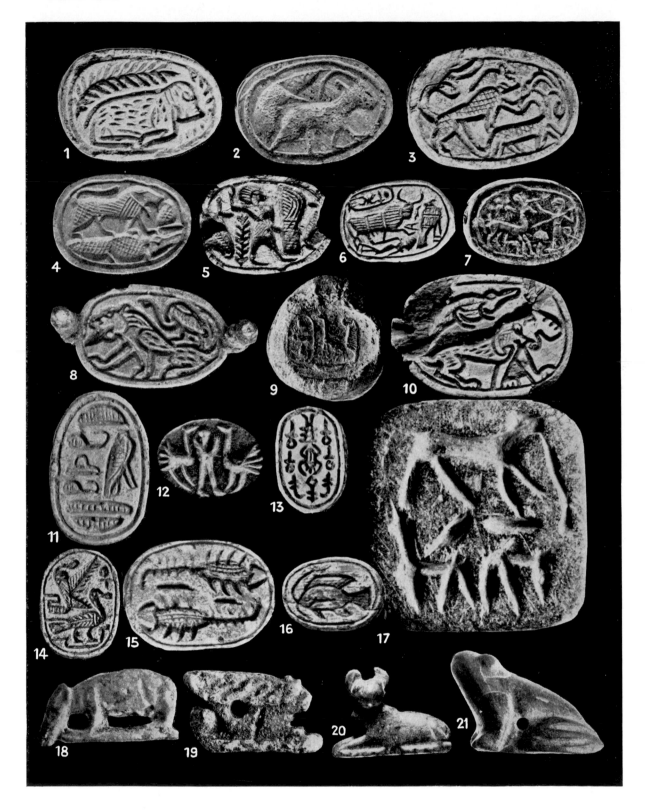

PLATE XVII

PLATE XVIII

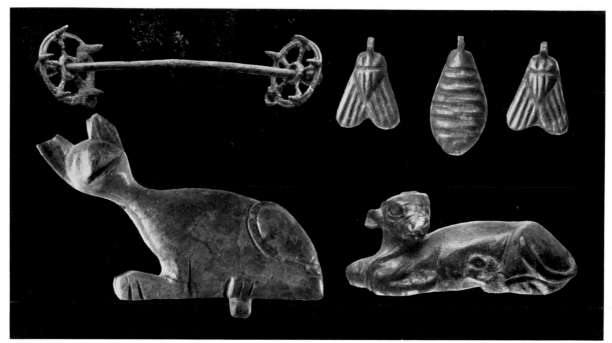

A.

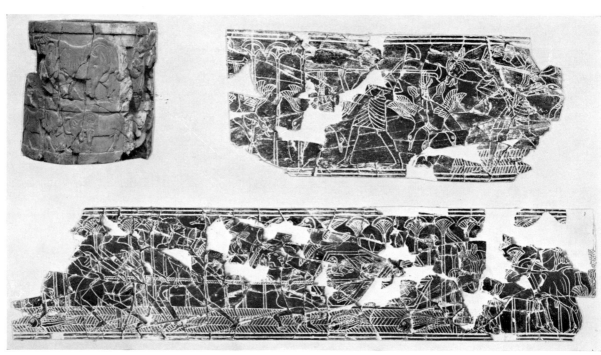

B.

PLATE XIX

PLATE XX

PLATE XXI

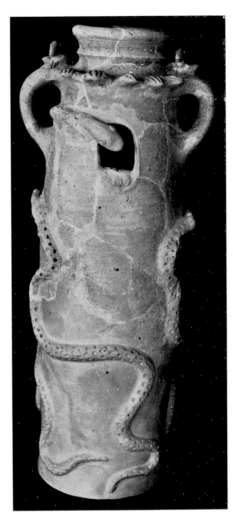

A.   B.

PLATE XXII

1.

2.

A.

B.

1.

2.

3.

4.

5.

6.

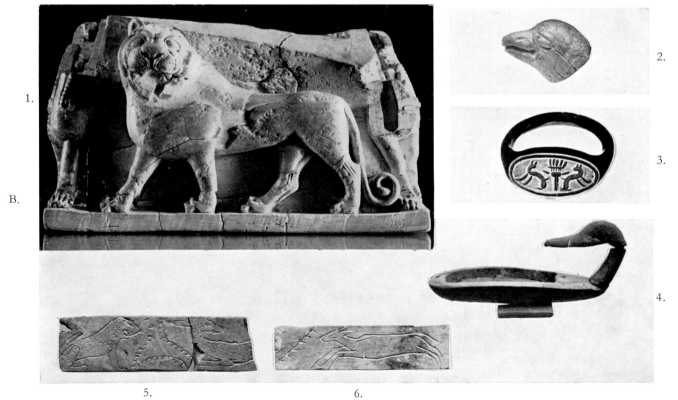

PLATE XXIII A

PLATE XXIII B

PLATE XXIV

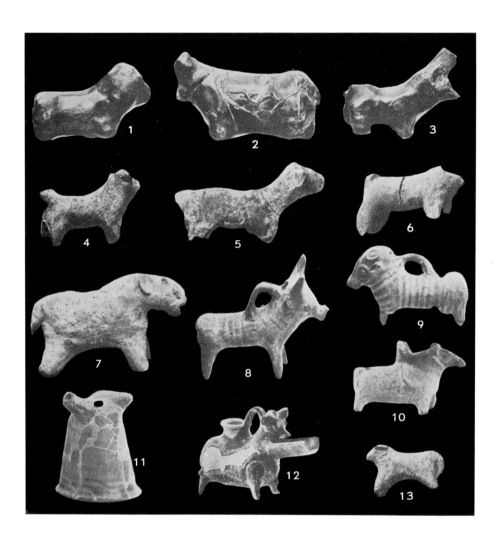

PLATE XXV

A.

B.

Plate XXVI

Plate XXVII

A.

B.